I Wond...
Reasons Why You !

M000117317

Maureen Mecozzi and Lisa Chesters

Contents

Rigby
A Harcourt Achieve Imprint

www.Rigby.com
1-800-531-5015

Why do I sneeze?

Imagine something tickles the inside of your nose, like a bit of dust. When this happens, a message is sent to the brain's sneeze center. The sneeze center then sends a message to muscles. Your stomach and chest muscles, muscles at the back of your throat, and your **diaphragm** all help produce a sneeze.

brain

throat muscles

chest muscles

stomach muscles

diaphragm

AHH-CHOO!

AHH-CHOO!

With a big push, that dust is moved out of your nose as fast as up to 100 miles per hour!

What causes a sneeze? Dust, cold air, and pepper are a few things. They can tickle the inside of the nose. This causes you to sneeze.

Fun Fact

Did you know that you can't keep your eyes open when you sneeze? It's true. Our eyes close every time we sneeze.

Why do I get dizzy?

Your ears are not only for hearing, but also for keeping your balance! There are three parts of your ear: outer, middle, and inner. The inner ear is the part that helps you to keep your balance.

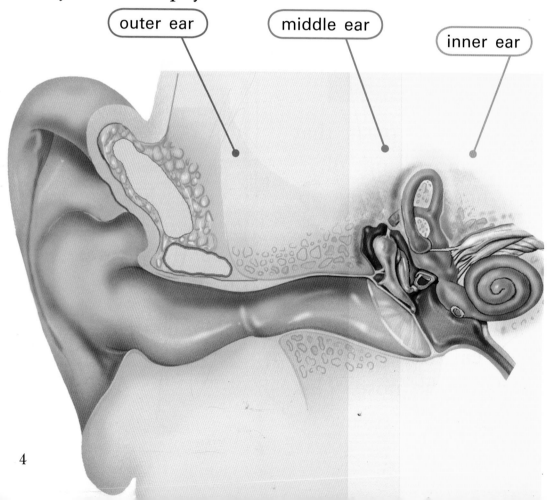

outer ear

middle ear

inner ear

Your inner ear has three **canals** that are filled with liquid and tiny hairs. When you move your head, the liquid inside moves the tiny hairs. A message is sent to your brain about the position of your head. Your brain then sends a message to the right muscles to keep you balanced.

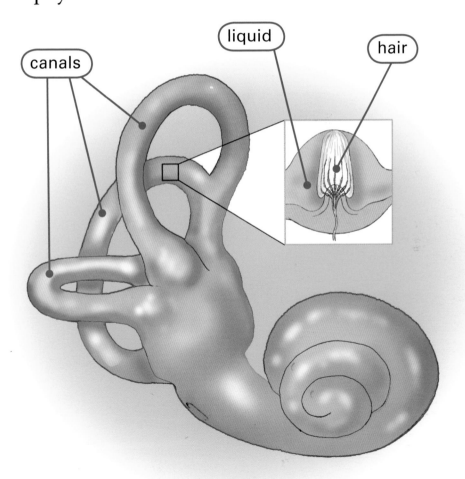

Think about the last time you spun yourself in circles. You may have felt dizzy when you suddenly stopped spinning. That's because the liquid in the canals kept moving after you stopped moving. When the liquid in your inner ear stops moving, your brain gets a message that says you're balanced again. Suddenly you're not dizzy anymore.

Why does my stomach make noises?

Your stomach makes an **acid** juice to **digest** food. This juice helps breaks down your food. If you eat too much fatty food, eat too fast, or skip a meal, your stomach makes too much juice. That extra juice moves around inside and causes your stomach to make noises.

acid

bits of food

stomach

7

Why do I yawn?

Everyone yawns, but nobody seems to know why for sure. Some think that when people are tired, their breathing is not as deep. So yawning would help get extra **oxygen** in the lungs. Others think that yawning helps to stretch the lungs.

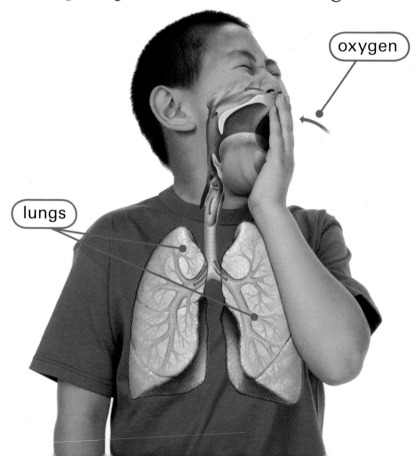

oxygen

lungs

Did you ever notice that if you yawn, others might yawn as well? One yawn seems to spread to others. But the reason why this happens is a mystery.

Why do I get goose bumps?

If you are ever outside in the cold too long, your body will shiver and get goose bumps. This is your body's way of telling you, "I'm cold. So warm me up."

BRRR!

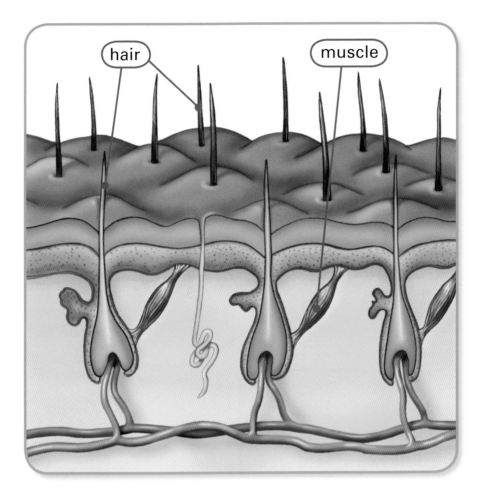

Every hair on your body has a tiny muscle just below the skin. When you get cold, those muscles tighten and pull on the hairs. The hairs stand straight up. Then your skin gets little bumps. These are called goose bumps. Once you get warm, your muscles relax and the goose bumps disappear.

Why do I get hiccups?

Almost everyone has had the hiccups at one time or another. Many different things cause hiccups. Eating too quickly or feeling nervous or excited can cause hiccups. Often it is difficult to get rid of the hiccups.

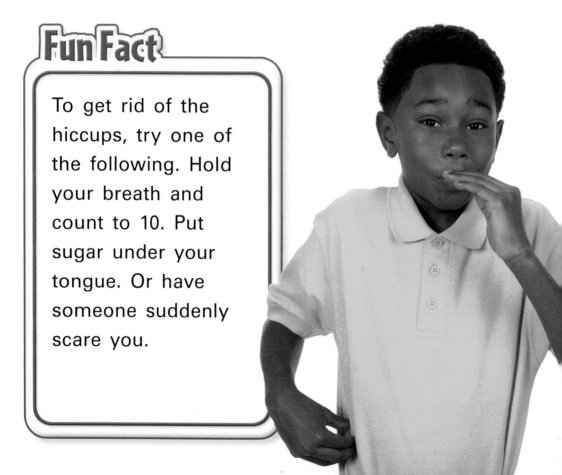

Fun Fact

To get rid of the hiccups, try one of the following. Hold your breath and count to 10. Put sugar under your tongue. Or have someone suddenly scare you.

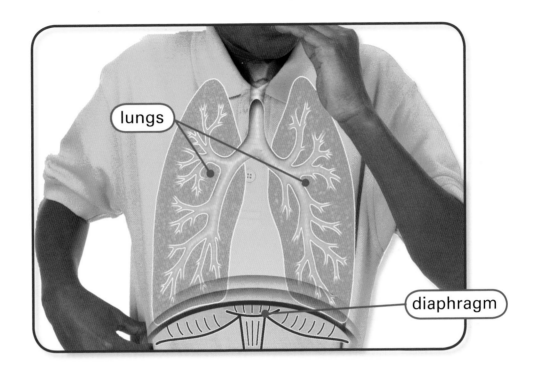

lungs

diaphragm

Hiccups start in your diaphragm. This is the muscle found near the bottom of your chest. This muscle pulls down when you breathe in and pushes up when you breathe out. The diaphragm almost always works perfectly, but sometimes you do something that bothers it, such as eating too fast. Suddenly the diaphragm will send up a breath when you don't expect it. Then out come the hiccups.

Why do my fingers and toes get wrinkly?

If you are in a bathtub or pool too long, you will probably notice your fingers and toes get wrinkly.

That's because the sebum on your skin washes away. Sebum is **invisible** oil on your skin. It keeps your skin safe from water. If you spend a long time in water, the sebum washes away and water soaks into your skin.

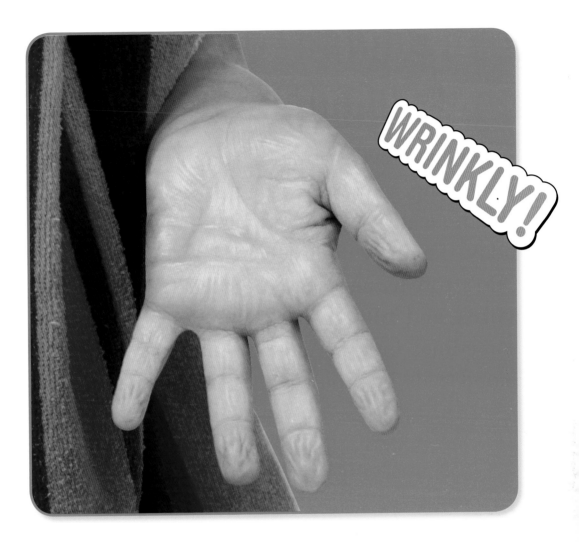

WRINKLY!

The extra water in your fingers and toes causes some parts of the skin to **swell**. Soon the skin on your fingers and toes wrinkles. When you dry out, the sebum returns and the wrinkles disappear.

Why do I get black and blue marks?

If you've ever bumped your leg against something, you may have felt a sharp pain and noticed a black and blue mark on your body. This is called a bruise. When your skin's soft tissue is bumped hard, small **veins** and **blood vessels** under the skin sometimes break. When they break, red blood cells leak out. This causes a bruise.

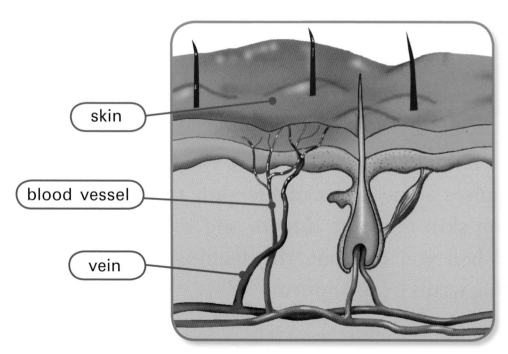

skin

blood vessel

vein

The bruise will probably go through colorful changes as days go by. All people bruise differently because we all have different types of skin.

Why do I get a headache when I eat cold food?

Have you ever had "brain freeze" when you eat ice cream? When you eat something cold and it touches the roof of your mouth in the very center, the blood vessels in your head sometimes swell up. This causes a headache that only lasts a minute or so.

You can keep from getting "brain freeze" by eating cold foods slowly. You can also hold your tongue up against the roof of your mouth when you eat a spoonful of something cold. By doing this, you'll warm up the cold food a bit, and you'll avoid a bad case of "brain freeze."

Why do my eyes water?

If you have ever gone for a walk on a windy day, you may have noticed that your eyes started to water. Your eyes were making tears, just like when you cry. Tears keep your eyes wet, which keeps your eyes safe. The tears wash out objects like dust that might be blowing in the wind.

Tear **glands** found above your eye let out the tears. And the **tear ducts** on the inside edge of each eye help the tears flow from your eyes. When your tear ducts are full, then tears flow down your face.

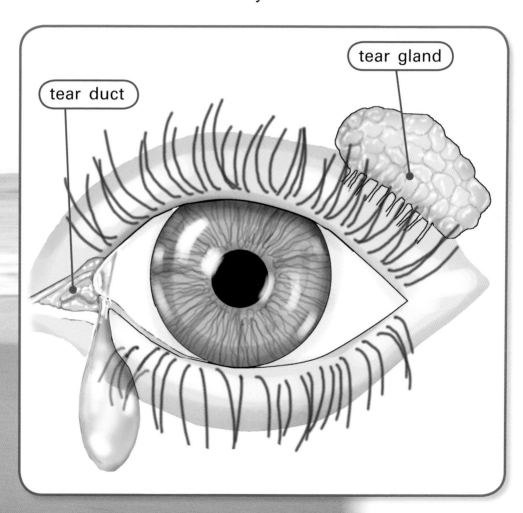

tear gland

tear duct

Got another question about your body?

Search for a book at the library or use the Internet to help you find the answer.

Glossary

acid a digestive juice that breaks down food

blood vessels small tubes that move blood throughout the body

canal a tube with liquid inside

diaphragm a dome-shaped muscle at the bottom of the chest

digest to break down food into small parts

glands parts of the body that give off different kinds of liquid

invisible can't be seen

oxygen a gas in the air that we breathe

swell to grow in size

tear ducts a part of the eye where tears flow from your eyes

veins small tubes that carry blood back to the heart

Index